Laughter and Love

Written by Allison Bottke and Heather Gemmen
Illustrated by Matt Whitlock

The God Allows U-Turns Ministry

Along with the exciting children's books published by Cook Communications, we want to share with readers the entire scope of the powerful God Allows U-Turns ministry of hope and healing. The broad outreach of this ministry includes the book you now hold in your hands, as well as a series of true short-story anthologies called *God Allows U-Turns, True Stories of Hope and Healing*. Multiple volumes in the popular compilation series are now available at bookstores internationally.

Bible book covers, back packs, ball caps, greeting cards, calendars, and more all bear the recognizable U-Turns road sign logo. The "New Direction Tour" featuring speakers, music, and more is also in the planning stages with the first event premiering in 2004 in a major USA city to be announced. Additionally, a cable television interview talk show, hosted by Allison Bottke, will soon be coming to homes around the world called: God Allows U-Turns—Real People, Real Issues, Real Faith, featuring interviews with people who have made dramatic U-turns.

For updates on the expanding ministry visit the God Allows U-Turns web site at http://www.godallowsuturns.com or write to Allison Bottke at: P.O. Box 717, Faribault, MN 55021-0717.

God Allows U-Turns for Kids
Laughter and Love
Picnics and Peace
Jingles and Joy

God Allows U-Turns for Youth
Friend or Freak
Pastrami Project
Get Real!

A faith parenting guide can be found on page 32.

Tyler ran in with a grin
with yellow smeared under his chin.
He clutched in his fist
what no mom can resist
and will stick to her shirt with a pin.

"What a good little boy is my Ty!
What a loveable, squeezable guy.
That we love one another,
both neighbor and mother,
is a law made by someone on high."

5

From happiness Tyler was reeling.
Mom's tickles soon made him start squealing.
God's law would be fun
and so easily done.
He loved feeling the way he was feeling.

Then Jessie peeked round by the door.
(She's his sister who just had turned four.)
"I want the flower!"
And Tyler got sour.
He did something that made Jessie sore.

11

Mom's smile turned into a frown.
Her eyes turned a much deeper brown.
"We love one another,
both *sister* and mother."
And someone got told to sit down.

13

TYLER!

Ty wanted to run far away.
He wanted to hit and to say,
"You're always so mean,
the meanest I've seen."
He hated to feel this way.

Mommy just kissed him and smiled.
"You're still a very sweet child.
Now where should this go
to help it to grow
the same as it did in the wild?"

But Tyler looked down with a pout.
He squirmed and he twisted about.
He knew it was bad,
but he was still mad.
So guess who pointed it out.

JESSIE!

The clock showed that Ty's time was through.
Mommy asked him what he would now do.
"First you showed love
then you gave Jess a shove.
Which way feels better to you?"

Tyler didn't take long to think.
Mom hardly had time to blink.
He looked at his sister.
He leaned in and kissed her.
"Let's go find a flower that's pink."

The fruit of the Spirit is...

LOVE...

Galatians 5:22

Laughter and Love

Life Issue: I want my children to make a U-turn toward a life of love.

Spiritual Building Block: Love

Do the following activities to help your children develop love as a fruit of the Spirit:

Sight: Go to the park or an indoor play-place with your children. On the way, invite your kids to play a game: your goal will be to find the people who are acting in love. Each time you or your children see someone who is living out love, you get to do the secret signal: maybe a sneeze, maybe a wink, maybe fingers through your hair. Later, do the secret signal whenever you see your kids live out love.

Sound: When you tuck your kids in at night, pray blessing over them. Out loud, thank God for loving your children so much and for wanting them to spend eternity with him. After you are done praying, ask your kids if they have asked Jesus to come into their hearts. If they haven't, invite them to do that. Tell them they have made a U-turn from a life without God to a life with God. Be assured that with the Spirit working in them, the fruit of love will grow.

Touch: Living out love is not something that comes naturally to anyone, not even for your children who have made a U-turn to a life with God. Love is a fruit of the Spirit: in other words, it comes because of the Spirit living and working in us. Encourage your children to spend time praying every day; remind them to invite the Spirit to help them to love others. And be sure to model loving behavior to your children.